SET 4 LIFE

FOUR AMAZINGLY SIMPLE STEPS TO PERSONAL, FINANCIAL, AND REFERRAL MARKETING SUCCESS

Tim R. Green

TESTIMONIALS

"Entrepreneurs looking to grow their business by referral and enjoy the process will be excited to read what Tim Green has to share. Tim has a remarkable skill to communicate effective referral marketing tactics in a simple manner that produces results."
Mike Macedonio, New York Times Best Selling Author and President of the Referral Institute

"Tim Green knows that when a system is simplified, it's more likely to be used. It's clear that the four proven steps outlined in this book will dramatically change how you think about your business and your life. Prepare yourself for unimaginable success."
Michelle R. Donovan, Referrability Expert and Best Selling Author of *The 29% Solution*

"Having personally followed Tim Green's four step system and achieved success in my own life, I am excited this is now in book form. There are many people who can use this system to break out of their own personal "rut" and stretch themselves to do and be more. Tim is truly a world-class trainer, networker and mentor who loves what he does and lives to serve others."
Asa Davis, Relationship Marketing Expert and Owner of Second Look Communications

"Would you rather succeed an average of 1 to 2 Percent of the time or 75 to 80 Percent of the time? Tim's book teaches you how to increase your closing success rate an average of 7,500% through referral marketing!!"
Scott Seifferlein, PGA Golf Guru, Owner of GrandRapidsGolfLesson.com
Stop Slicing Five Swings Guaranteed!

ISBN # 978-0-615-40892-7

Printed in the United States of America.

SET 4 LIFE

FOUR AMAZINGLY SIMPLE STEPS TO PERSONAL, FINANCIAL, AND REFERRAL MARKETING SUCCESS

Learn how to
"Predict your income by predicting
your Referrals for Life®"
in four simple steps

Tim R. Green

TABLE OF CONTENTS

FOREWORD

I salute you for picking up the book you now hold in your hands. I'm a huge believer in the power that referrals can bring when they are a daily part of your marketing efforts. Regardless of good or challenging economic times, in my expert opinion, referrals are hands down the most effective way for anyone to build his or her business or non-profit organization.

When I learned that Tim was going to write a book on financial, personal, and referral marketing success, I was excited for a variety of reasons. First, I've witnessed his training skills in action and have seen the powerful strategies he teaches. Second, what he advocates has produced astounding results not only with other clients, but also within my own company.

I'd like to share with you a little history and background as to why I'm so strongly endorsing this powerful and relevant book. Having written several bestselling books on the topics of sales, marketing, and motivation, along with reading an average of two to three books per week over the last several years, I've made it my mission to learn from the top leaders, past and present, in the business arena.

With ease and supreme confidence, I can tell you that Tim Green ranks right up there with many of today's masters, such as Bob Burg and Tim Templeton, when it comes to the topics of networking and referral marketing. Tim is fortunate to have as his mentor the world's top referral marketing expert, Dr. Ivan Misner of the Referral Institute. Yes, Tim is in very good company. This book will now awaken the globe and serve as proof that a new agent of positive change has joined their ranks.

What you'll quickly discover within these pages is that Tim moves beyond theory to deliver a powerful blueprint for how to effectively give and receive referrals. He takes the "accidental referral" that most people get and explains why this is just the tip of the iceberg. In addition, he points out a multitude of ways that referrals can be given and received by others. I must admit, several of his tips I'd never been exposed to or had even heard about until reading through the manuscript. This is a huge bonus and pleasant surprise for those of us continually looking to raise our game.

Here's the danger with this book: Tim makes it so easy to use the powerful strategies contained that some readers will skim through the book and be tempted to assume they already know it all. In fact, that's also the blessing of the book. If you take action and apply what he recommends, you will begin to see additional referrals, better relationships, increased sales, visibility, and higher profits.

You should also know that the book you now possess is a steal compared to what Tim's students and speaking clients gladly pay to work with him directly. I've often said that a well written book by an expert is the best deal on the planet. This book could command a much higher fee, as Tim's students and happy clients can attest, but luckily for us he has taken the time to break down his success formula within these pages. You and I are now much richer for it.

Read this book once and highlight key points. Read it again and take action on what you plan to apply immediately. Go through it a third time to see how many of the new changes have positively impacted your business, life, but more importantly, your growing bottom line!

Tony Rubleski - August 2010 Bestselling author of the Mind Capture series www.MindCaptureGroup.com

ACKNOWLEDGMENTS

This book would never have been written without the people in my life who pushed me. First of all, I want to thank Tony Rubleski, who sat down with me on a cold, snowy day one December. I shared my goal of going out nationwide presenting my four steps to financial, personal, and referral marketing success. Tony said, "Great, so when are you going to write your book?" If he hadn't encouraged me to write this book, it never would have happened.

Lisa Mininni, for assisting me in coming up with the title of the book and contributing to this book by writing the closing chapter, It's Your Choice. She is a Referral Institute Referrals for Life® student who has adopted the principles of this book to create phenomenal success. Her input is invaluable.

Dr. Ivan Misner, Founder, and Mike Macedonio, President, of Referral Institute. The referral marketing section of this book could never have been written if not for their superior knowledge of the subject and the material they created for Referral Institute.

Rose Hackbarth for creating a transcript of my Referral Success 202 four hour workshop which was used to create this book. She spent countless hours going over my recording of the workshop to create the transcript. The book would never have been written without the transcript she created.

My brother, David Lynch, a fantastic graphic artist who designed the book jacket and the illustrations in this book.

Asa Davis, who assisted me in writing this book and ensured that my grammar is correct.

My very close friends John & Karen Conover for their tremendous support. They tell everyone "No matter how tough it gets, Tim is like a cat and will always land on his feet!"

My very talented daughter, Morgan, who gave her knowledge and creative input in the design and content of this book. She never allows us to settle for less than the best; she is my daughter, and my friend.

My sons, Chris, for dancing to his own beat and helping me be a freer thinker; Joey, for his sense of humor, always making me find the funny side of life; Ryan, who is gone too soon in life but never in spirit; and Justin, a fantastic father and businessman I look up to, who has amazing humor and energy.

My daughter-in-law, Sarah, whom I respect and cannot thank enough for keeping me in check and *un*balanced.

My Dad, for instilling in me the resolve to never give up pursuing my dreams in life, and the work ethic needed to live the life I have.

My grandsons, Kalib, who keeps me on my toes and a smile in my heart. Braylon, to whom I say, on record, "Grandpa will be your agent in life." The bond we have is no accident.

My wife and best friend, Karen, the love of my life, who loves and supports me and always believes in me and my love of helping others achieve their dreams.

I am truly grateful to everyone that I have mentioned. Because of their role in this book, lives will be changed!

Tim R. Green

INTRODUCTION FROM THE AUTHOR

I have read a lot of books that promise more success and money. The problem is that to achieve the goal promised by many of these books, you have to try and implement complex strategies. I think life is way too complex already, and it doesn't need to be.

My goal is to help you "Predict your income by predicting your Referrals for Life®" by making success a very simple process.

How is this book going to accomplish this?

I'll teach you the four steps to personal, financial, and referral marketing success and how referral marketing can take your business to a whole new level.

CHAPTER ONE

IT'S ALL YOUR FAULT

Upon conducting research on referral marketing, Dr. Ivan Misner, considered to be the world's top expert in networking and referrals, found that only 3% of businesses are actively engaged and immersed in referral marketing. Yet if you ask someone what the best form of marketing is, the response you get is, "Word of mouth marketing." The following story gives insight into the current business mindset and why I wrote this book.

Sue, a financial advisor, came to my office on hot, blistery day to discuss the training programs Referral Institute offers. She considered herself a master networker because she was constantly giving referrals. In fact, because she is financial advisor, she was able to provide a lot of referrals to an insurance agent. In 2009, the insurance agent made a six figure income solely from the referrals Sue provided him.

This was her dilemma: she gave a lot of referrals but did not receive referrals in return. Sue said if I could solve this for her, she would join Referral Institute's Referrals for Life® training program. Sue waited for me to give her the answer.

I told her it was all her fault.

Sue looked so mad, I thought she was going to stand up and leave. Instead, she started arguing with me and said that apparently I was not listening to her. She said, "I give at least four to five referrals a week and receive nothing in return." I asked her if she set the expectation up front that she expected referrals in return. She said no, that people should already know she expects referrals in return.

I educated Sue as to why she truly wasn't getting referrals and shared with her my four step system. In the next twelve months, Sue produced record sales for her business because she adopted the four step system.

Sue developed a relationship with a new insurance agent who understood the need to give referrals back to her. As a result of a referral from the insurance agent, Sue landed one of the largest 401(k) plans in the history of her company. Because she had false notions about the relationship she had with the original insurance agent, Sue was missing out on opportunities to receive referrals.

Chapter Two

System Smart

When you look at the string of letters below, what do you see?

OPPORTUNITYISNOWHERE

Many people see the above as "Opportunity is nowhere." For some, it reads "Opportunity is now here." If the former is the how you see it, you may be in a rut. My job is to help you get out of that rut by showing you some new ideas.

If you are not waking up each day with drive and enthusiasm to take your business to the next level, you could be in a rut. Implementing just one or two new things can get you out of your rut for a day.

Jim Rohn was a well-known entrepreneur, author, and motivational speaker who influenced many other influential people, such as Anthony Robbins, Mark Victor Hansen, Jack Canfield, and Brian Tracy. Jim became successful in the self development field before it became popular. Jim Rohm believed that if you don't immerse yourself in learning with books, CDs, and classes, you will get into a rut.

Muhammad Ali is considered by many to be the greatest heavyweight boxer of all time. One interesting fact about Ali is that he correctly predicted the outcome of many of his

bouts. For 17 of 19 fights, Ali correctly predicted both the round and the outcome.

How was he able to do this? He had a system. He studied and understood the weaknesses of his opponents. Ali invested time and money to know how to beat every other boxer.

To avoid getting yourself into a rut, you must have a system that will ensure your success. Jim Rohn said you need to get into a program that has 100% predictability of success.

Let's walk through how a system's approach can predict your results.

1. Write down a number between 1 and 9 (this takes a little math, but only a little, I promise).

2. Multiply that number by 9.

3. If it is a single digit, leave it alone. If it is a 2-digit number, add them together to get a single digit.

4. Take that number and subtract 5.

5. Determine what letter of the alphabet corresponds to that number. For instance, if the number is 1, the letter is A; if 2, then B; If 3, the C, etc.

6. Now that you have the letter, think of a country whose name starts with that letter.

7. Then take the 2nd letter of that country name and think of a 4-legged animal whose name starts with that letter.

Did you think of Denmark and either an elephant or an elk? Remember: an emu has two legs.

Am I psychic? How did I know the country and animal you would think of? Because I have a system with 100% predictability of success. To be successful, you have to have a system that is predictable.

Do you have a predictable system for generating quality referrals?

Before we discuss referrals and help you "Predict your income by predicting your Referrals for Life®," we need to cover the four steps to personal, financial, and referral marketing success.

Chapter Three

The Story of the 4 Steps

A friend of mine by the name of John was laid off after working for 25 years for Delphi in Flint, MI. John received a severance package from Delphi and was sent on his way into early retirement. Because of his positive attitude, John saw this as "Opportunity Is Now Here."

Since he was a little boy, John always wanted to be a farmer. Having been laid off with no opportunity to return to his old workplace, John was able to pursue his life's dream. Remember: a change or ending is always a beginning.

You may be unaware of this, but 80% of the working population in America does not like what they are doing for a living. You may be reading this and not like what you are doing.

John realized this was his opportunity to become a farmer. He wanted to become a farmer as soon as possible. What do you think he purchased? That's right, *a farm*.

See how this works? If you want to become a locksmith, you buy a locksmith business. If you want to become an underwater basket weaver, you buy an underwater basket weaving business.

Having no experience but an awful lot of passion, John spent $500,000 on his farm and moved to Northern Wisconsin to begin working on it. Before he did that, however, he asked me about what I've adopted in my life to help make me more successful. Here are the four simple steps to personal, financial, and referral marketing success:

1. **Believe in yourself.**
2. **Have the right vehicle.**
3. **Be consistent.**
4. **Be persistent.**

After purchasing the farm, John began to review the four steps. He said to himself, "I must believe in myself. I just spent half a million dollars on this farm!" He knew he was moving in the right direction. He had a little trouble with #2, though. John wasn't sure if he should raise crops, raise sheep, or something else.

John toured his farm after the purchase was complete and walked into the barn. As he was inspecting the barn, looking for ideas, he tripped over something. John looked down and said, "Wow, I can't believe this. It's a pig!" A female pig, no less. He said, "This must be a sign from above that I'm supposed to be a pig farmer." But John had one obstacle to overcome if he wanted to expand his pig farm. Did you guess it? He needed to find a male pig somewhere.

John reviewed the four steps again. He felt certain he had accomplished steps #1 & #2, but he needed some help with #3. John needed to find a successful system and follow it consistently. He also needed a mentor who had followed the system and been successful. John decided he needed to find the top pig farmer around, and he was willing to travel as far as he needed to find him.

John searched all over the state of Wisconsin looking for the top pig farmer in the state. As it turned out, the top pig farmer in the entire state of Wisconsin was only five miles down the road from John's new farm! What luck! John immediately called the farmer and asked if he could bring over his female pig. The farmer said, "No problem at all. In fact, I have so much business, it would be nice if there were another farmer I could partner with."

John was elated. But there was one problem: getting the pig to the other farm.

Have you ever tried to walk a pig? Where do they go? That's right, everywhere EXCEPT where you want them to go. They are a stubborn animal.

John asked the farmer, "How am I going to get my pig down to your farm?"

"Very simple," the farmer replied. "There are 2 tools you'll need. Do you have a pick-up truck?"

John said, "Yes, I have a pick-up truck."

"Do you have a wheelbarrow?" asked the farmer.

"Yes, I have a wheelbarrow," replied John.

"Great," the farmer said, "this is what I want you to do, John. I want you to lift the wheelbarrow straight up and

down, and then set the wheelbarrow by the pig's rear end and push down. This will cause the pig to slide to the middle of the wheelbarrow, balancing her weight. Then, wheel her up into the pick-up truck, leave her in the wheelbarrow for easy unloading and drive her down to my farm."

John was in shock at the simplicity. He said, "You have to be kidding me. It's that simple?"

The farmer replied, "How do you think I became the best, by working harder or by working smarter?"

So John went out to the barn and did exactly as the farmer described. He lifted the wheelbarrow straight up and down, then set the wheelbarrow by the pig's rear end and pushed down. Lo and behold, that pig slipped right to the middle of the wheelbarrow, balancing her weight. He then wheeled her up into the pick-up truck, left her in the wheelbarrow, and drove down to the farm.

Once John unloaded his pig at the other farm, he asked the farmer how he would know if his pig had become pregnant. "That's easy," said the farmer, "it was in the Farmer's Almanac a few years back, and it works every time. Tomorrow morning, at the crack of dawn, you have to jump out of your bed, run over to your bedroom window, and look outside. If the pig is rolling in the mud, it means the pig is pregnant. If the pig is rolling in the straw, the pig is not pregnant."

That night, John was so excited he had found the #1 system and the #1 mentor that he stayed up all night tossing and turning in anticipation. He knew in the morning he would have a pregnant pig and would be able to start his pig farm.

John jumped out of bed at the crack of dawn and ran over to the bedroom window. He looked out the window and saw the pig rolling in straw.

"How could this be?" John asked himself. He remembered the four steps to success. Believe in yourself, have the right vehicle, be consistent, and BE PERSISTENT. He knew he had to take the pig to the farm again or else he would never have a pregnant pig. "Be persistent," John said to himself. John immediately called the farmer and asked if he could bring the pig down again. "Sure," said the farmer. "The pigs rarely get pregnant on the first try."

Did you know most people give up after only the *third* try? It's too bad, because sometimes people are closer to success than they think, and they give up too soon.

John knew he needed to be persistent. He went right out and lifted the wheelbarrow straight up and down. He set the wheelbarrow right by the pig's rear end and pushed down. The pig slipped right to the middle of the wheelbarrow, balancing her weight. He wheeled her up into the pick-up truck, left her in the wheelbarrow and drove down to the farm.

That night, before he went to bed, John read a book. This book said if you truly want a positive outcome, you need to have positive input. John decided he needed to make sure he was always thinking positive thoughts. John sat up the entire night on the end of his bed repeating, "I know this pig's going to be rolling in the mud. I know the pig is going to be pregnant." He took it one step further and visualized the pig rolling in the mud.

After the second straight night of no sleep, John jumped out of bed at the crack of dawn, ran over to the window and looked out. The pig was rolling in the straw. John said, "I can't believe this! I've had two nights of no sleep, and the pig is still not pregnant. I'm going to give it one more chance and if this pig is still not pregnant, I'm moving on to sheep herding."

John repeated his system of getting the pig into his truck and drove down to the farm. "This had better work," John said to himself.

That night John fell into a deep sleep. He had already given up, so there was no excitement or anticipation to keep him awake. At 8 o'clock in the morning, his wife woke him up, shouting, "Honey, are you going to see if the pig is pregnant?"

"Naw," John said. "I've decided to take up sheep herding.

Could you do me a favor, though? Go look out the window and tell me what that pig is doing."

John's wife just shook her head. "Isn't this wonderful," she said. "You spent half a million dollars on this farm, dragged me out of the city to the middle of nowhere, and now I've got to be the one to see if we're going to be successful or not. Fine."

She walked over to the window, looked out, and exclaimed, "Oh my gosh! You're not going to believe this!"

John jumped out of bed, ran over to the window and said, "What is it? Is the pig rolling in the mud?"

"No," she replied. "The pig is sitting in the wheelbarrow."

I've put together a simple four step system to help you achieve success.

But let me point this out: you have to follow each step or else it won't work. Many people aren't persistent enough and give up just before they have achieved success. You have to follow each step carefully if you want this to work for you. I promise that if you follow this system, you will achieve whatever you put your mind to.

"You must do the thing you think you cannot do."
— Eleanor Roosevelt

STEP ONE:

BELIEVE IN YOURSELF

CHAPTER FOUR

BELIEVE THAT YOU CAN

When we're young, we think we can do anything. Ask any 7 or 8 year old, and they will tell you what they want to be when they grow up: doctor, ballerina, scientist, firefighter. They assume they can do anything they want, because they don't know differently.

Something happens, though, when we get older. We lose that belief that anything is possible, that we can be or do anything.

Can't = Will Not

Recently, I discovered something that opened my eyes about what holds us back in life. When we say "I cannot," what we are really saying is "I WILL not." You might be saying, "I cannot follow a four step system to achieve financial success." Or, "I cannot take the time to attend a seminar or read a book." What you are really saying is, "I will not" do those things.

You know what I am talking about if you have children. Have you ever asked a child to clean his room? What is the typical response? "I can't!" right? What he is really saying is, "I will not clean my room." He can clean his room. He just chooses not to do it.

Do you believe in yourself? Do you surround yourself with people who support you?

Your passion is what proves that you do believe in yourself. To use a sports analogy, the person who believes in himself goes for the ball. He also has his teammates help him to get the ball. Do you have passion for what you do? Are you going for the ball? Do you have teammates who are there to support you?

Consider the tuna, the shark, and the dolphin. Do you know why tuna exist? They exist solely to be eaten, in many cases, by sharks. Quite an existence, don't you think? Sharks are the ultimate marine predator, one of the few species to be feared even by man.

Sharks rarely attack dolphins. Sharks are faster than dolphins (2-3 times) and are far more ferocious. Why is it then that sharks avoid contact with something they could generally overtake?

Because dolphins travel together in pods. If a shark attacks a dolphin and the rest of pack is nearby, the other dolphins retaliate against the shark. They use their tails to whip the shark or will use their nose to ram the shark under the jaw, killing it. Dolphins rely on one another to deal with a dangerous situation.

In your business, which one of the three are you?

5

Are you a tuna, waiting to be gobbled up by the competition?

Are you a shark, out there alone trying to get whatever business you can?

Or are you a dolphin? If you are utilizing referral marketing, helping others grow their businesses and training them to help you, then you are a dolphin. You have a team of people assembled to handle an attack from those sharks out there.

If you believe in yourself, others around you will also believe in you. They will want you to succeed as much as you want it.

When choosing people for your "pod," you must be selective. Jim Rohn said, "You are an average of the five people you spend the most time with."

Other people can influence our activity and behavior. If you perceive yourself as a positive person but hang around negative people, you will become negative. Spend time

6

with people who have accomplished what you want to accomplish, and you will get where you want to go in life. Rohn also said, "… your income [is] the average of the five people you hang around the most."

If you want to make $100,000, hang around people who make at least that much money. If you want to be a millionaire, hang around with millionaires, or at least meet them, read their books or attend their seminars.

A lot of people go to seminars, read books or listen to CDs, hoping to improve their lives. Some are able to make changes to improve their status in life, while others fall back into their old habits. Albert Einstein said, "Insanity is doing the same thing over and over again expecting different results." We must make changes in order to get out of our rut.

The economy is rough; the current state of the economy is the worst it has been since the Great Depression. We need to do something different if we want more success.

With the economy as bad as it is, though, would you agree there is someone in your profession who will make a lot of money this year? Maybe even have their best year ever? Yes, the economy is bad and people are more cautious about spending their money. But the money is out there, and people are actually spending it, despite what the newspapers tell us. You need to be sure to get your fair share.

If you want to get different results, you have to change something you are doing now. For some people, investing in a new kind of training may make the difference.

CHAPTER FIVE

INVEST IN YOURSELF

If you believe in yourself, you invest in yourself. Tiger Woods is a great example of this. Tiger is one of the greatest golfers of all time. Some say he was born to play golf.

Did you know that Tiger Woods invests over $1,000,000 per year on his golf swing? He has coaches who follow him everywhere to videotape and analyze his swing. He invested his earnings in his formative years on learning and coaching to develop his game. He spent money on his own training, working to perfect the game of golf.

Has it worked? You tell me: he is considered to be the greatest golfer in the world. In May 2009, Forbes magazine estimated that Tiger Woods' total net worth is **$600 million**. His career earnings total more than $1 billion.

I say it's working pretty well for him.

The top producers in any sport or business understand the value of continual learning. You may be #1 now, but someone else who wants it more and is willing to put in the time, effort, and money necessary to be the best may overtake you. Top athletes know that you must be in top physical and mental condition in order to be the best in a sport.

Many top athletes are aware of this formula, but most people have never seen a mathematical formula for success. It is quite simple. Take your income and multiply it by 10%. This is how much you must invest in yourself on a regular basis.

FORMULA FOR SUCCESS

ANNUAL INCOME $_____ X 10%= $_____

To achieve what you want in life, invest at least 10% of your income in your own development. If you want to achieve half of what you want, invest 5%. If you don't want to achieve anything in life, invest 0%. It is that easy.

There is a direct correlation between how much we invest in our own learning and education and how successful we are in life.

We spend a lot of money on advertising, which is important. We spend a lot of money on cars, which are less important. We rarely spend money on ourselves. Then we wonder why our plans for success aren't working for us. We need to invest 10% of our income on ourselves each year through books, tapes, seminars and training programs in order to be successful.

How much are you spending on yourself right now? Are you above, at or below the 10% mark? Look for ways that you can better yourself through learning or training. Remember: if you are unwilling to make the investment necessary to achieve your full potential, someone else will accomplish what you want to accomplish.

REVIEW: Step One

STEP ONE: Believe in Yourself
- Believe That You Can
- Invest in Yourself

POINTS TO PONDER:

When faced with a challenge, how do you respond?

_____

_____

_____

_____

Who are the five people you spend the most time with?

_____

_____

_____

_____

How much are you investing in yourself and your education?

_____

_____

_____

_____

STEP TWO

HAVE THE RIGHT VEHICLE

CHAPTER SIX

PICK THE RIGHT VEHICLE

Would you like to drive the most expensive car in the world? The Bugatti Veyron sells for $2,044,000 U.S. (as of 2010). Only 30 of them are made each year, so good luck getting your hands on one.

Consider this: will a $30,000 car get you to the grocery store just as well as a Veyron? Sure. So, why do people buy such expensive cars? Prestige? Because they can? Yes and yes. It makes them feel good, because it projects a certain image. The vehicle is a means to an end.

If you were delivering 2x4s to a construction site, would you drive a $2,000,000+ car? Probably not. You need to identify the proper use for a vehicle.

Apply this concept to your marketing. Are you using the right vehicle to market your business?

You have numerous ways to advertise or market your products and services. Many people take the sawed off shotgun approach to marketing. That is, they spend a little bit on television ads, a little bit on radio, a little bit on direct mail, and so on. In the end, it all adds up to *a little bit*.

What is the most cost effective form of advertising? Word of mouth, yet most people invest little to no time in their referral marketing plan. Instead, they invest in methods that deliver cold leads.

The biggest investment you will make with referral marketing is that of time. This investment pays off, however. According to the US Chamber of Commerce, the average closing ratio for a referral is 75-85%, compared to 1-2% for a cold call. It makes more sense to me to spend your time receiving referrals instead of making cold calls.

CHAPTER SEVEN

REFERRALS

I have found that when my referral sources give me a referral, I have a much greater chance of closing a transaction.

Have you received referrals lately? I suppose you have, considering 98% of all businesses rely on referrals to gain new business, according to research by Dr. Ivan Misner.

Do you cold call? We all may have done it at some point in our careers. As I previously mentioned, on average, 1-2% of cold calls turn into business. If I know I need to close 10 deals every week, this means I need to get in contact with 500 people each week using cold calling.

In contrast, if someone sends you a referral, 75-85% of the time that turns into business. It is 40 times more likely that you will close a referral over a cold call. Again, if I need to close 10 deals every week, I need to get in contact with 12-14 people each week with referral marketing. Contacting 14 people instead of 500 people seems pretty manageable. Do you see how it becomes easier to "Predict your income by predicting your Referrals for Life®"?

Not every referral will close, because some might be bad referrals. Not all referrals are created equal. I can teach you how to turn bad referrals into good referrals.

Have you ever received a bad referral? Let's say that you can't get a hold of the person to whom you were referred. You call them repeatedly, and they never return your calls. Or, you call them and they have never heard of you or the referral source.

So, what do you do? You go back to the person who gave you the referral and ask for help. What does the referring person say? "Oh, just keep trying, and you'll get a hold of them?" You then try the prospect a few more times and give up.

Why does this happen? Because many people are not trained on how to give referrals. And those receiving the referrals are too afraid to ask for better quality referrals.

Referral training companies, like Referral Institute, teach people how to train referral sources to give them the quality of referral they want to receive. No more getting referrals that go nowhere. Students are taught to accept nothing less than a referral in which an appointment is already set.

If you're wondering if someone would actually set an appointment for you when they give you a referral, ask yourself if you would be willing to do the same for someone else. The quality of the referrals you receive is dependent on the quality of referrals you give. If you want to receive better quality referrals from your sources, give them better quality referrals.

Chapter Eight

Predicting Referrals

In the book *Truth or Delusion* (this is a must read book!), Dr. Ivan Misner and his coauthors bring up common misconceptions regarding networking and referral marketing. One common myth is that "You can't predict referrals."

This seems logical, right? How could someone possibly predict when another person is going to give him or her a referral?

The belief that you can't predict referrals is a delusion. You can predict referrals if you have a system. When you have a fully functioning referral marketing strategy in operation, you will know approximately how many referrals you can expect over a given period of time and of what quality those referrals will be.

The key is identifying other people who are willing and able to give you referrals. If you have an established relationship with someone and have a keen understanding of what will motivate that person to refer business to you, he or she will refer business to you.

The first thing you have to do is identify people who can and will refer business to you. One way to do this is to attend networking meetings in order to meet these people. Networking events can be a great way to meet other people, including potential clients and referral sources.

Truth or Delusion

The more networking meetings you go to, the better. This is a delusion. Going to networking events is important, but attending too many can get you nowhere. While it is important to be introduced to a wide array of contacts, you must also be sure to have depth in those relationships. If you attend too many events, you will be unable to attain quality, long-term relationships with others who can give you referrals.

There are three major types of networking groups you can get involved with in your business. The first type is a casual contact group. These are groups like chambers of commerce, business card exchanges, and after-hours mixers. The purpose of these groups is to get to meet other people in your community. Some of these people may be your competitors; others may be your clients or potential referral source. Attending casual contact networking events is a great way to establish a relationship with someone.

The second type of group is a service club. The purpose of a service club is, well, service to the community. Groups such as Rotary, Kiwanis, Jaycees and others provide you with the opportunity to give back to your community and get to know other businesspeople in the process. Rather than joining these groups for business, you join to give back. But you can generate quality relationships through activity in these service groups that can lead to future business.

The third type of group is a hard-contact networking group. This type of group meets on a regular basis for the sole purpose of generating referrals for one another, and unlike the casual contact and service groups, they only allow one person per profession. Go on the Internet and search for a hard-contact networking group in your area. This form of networking allows you to focus on business relationships with a small group of people to develop referral partners.

It is important that you be involved in all three types of networking groups in order to meet a wide variety of people and develop deep relationships with others. Each type of group has its benefits, so be selective about what you get involved in, so you can spend your time wisely.

Once you meet someone at a networking meeting, you'll need to determine whether or not he or she is a potential referral source for you. We'll discuss how to identify referral sources later in the book.

But wait. What about your clients? A client of yours could be your number one referral source. If you provide great customer service to your clients, after all, people will refer business to you, right? Wrong. This is yet another networking delusion.

Your customers expect great customer service, so providing that service will only gain you their personal business. There is no guarantee that they will recommend your services to their friends and family if you have merely met their minimum expectations. You have to find out what will motivate them to want to give you referrals on an ongoing basis.

Think about your clients. Has every single one of them given you a referral? Probably not. You may be the best of the best, and yet the referrals are far from raining in.

Do you know why they are not referring business to you? Because you are not asking. The more important question is, why are you not asking? The answer to that question lies in the VCP Process®.

"It isn't what you know or who you know, but how well you know them."

— Dr. Ivan Misner

CHAPTER NINE

THE VCP PROCESS®

Don't get me wrong, knowing people is important, and knowing a lot of people can be beneficial to you and your business. However, it is important that you establish deep, quality relationships in order to unlock the power of referral marketing.

The average person knows a lot of people, typically 250-500. You may know more or fewer. The key to maximizing these relationships and establishing a quality referral relationship lies in the VCP Process®, which we will outline shortly.

You will select referral partners from these 250-500 people, and you will train them to go out and create referrals for your business. If none of the people you already know can be quality referral partners with you, you will want to recruit others for these roles. Again, my goal is to help "Predict your income by predicting your Referrals for Life®." Finding the right referral partners is crucial to achieving this goal.

Referral partners are people who are going to give you referrals on a continual basis, because they are motivated to do so. These are people who will help you "Predict your income by predicting your Referrals for Life®."

If you are part of a networking group, especially a hard-contact networking group, you may think that everyone in the group is a referral source for you. This is another networking delusion. Only a limited number of people are going to have the ability and desire to give you referrals on an ongoing basis.

You will want to start with four people, either inside or outside of one of your networking groups, on whom you will focus. Go ahead and write the names of four people who you think could be long-term referral sources for you in the ovals next to the figures on the diagram on page 24. Your ability to get referrals from these people, or anyone for that matter, depends on where you are in the VCP Process®.

The VCP Process® is an assessment tool for measuring relationships. VCP stands for Visibility, Credibility, and Profitability. It basically tells you where you stand with a potential referral source.

If you have Visibility with someone, it means that person knows who you are and perhaps what you do for a living but knows nothing about the quality of products or services you provide. You may have met the person briefly, but if you were to call six weeks later, he or she will likely have forgotten who you are.

Some people go to networking events trying to collect as many business cards as they possibly can. They think this makes them a good networker and highly referable. All it really means is that they are good at collecting cards and gaining Visibility. This type of networking is about as good as cold calling.

Once you have Visibility with someone, you want to move to Credibility. This is the stage in the relationship in which another person is comfortable either doing business with you or passing referrals to you. Only when people feel you are credible will they pass you a referral, since their reputation is on the line.

You can have Credibility with someone, and yet he or she may stop passing you referrals. Why? Because you are unable to reach Profitability with that person.

Profitability is the stage in which the relationship is beneficial for both parties. In a reciprocal referral relationship, each party is passing an equitable number of referrals to each other. In order to be profitable, both parties must feel they are receiving value as a result of the relationship.

The important thing to remember with VCP is that it is a process. You must be visible before you can be credible; you must be credible before you can be profitable. Many people make the mistake of thinking they can jump right to Profitability. They think they can move directly into a reciprocal referral relationship. Moving correctly through the VCP Process® takes time and effort.

To identify referral sources, you want to move through the VCP Process®, and you must understand from where these referral sources may come.

CHAPTER TEN

EIGHT SOURCES OF REFERRALS

Referrals can come from anyone at any time. But there are certain groups of people who are more apt to give you referrals than others.

#1 – Members of your contact sphere

A contact sphere is a group of businesses that have the same target market but do not compete. People who are in your contact sphere are your best sources of referrals because they have the same type of client you have. If you train them on how to give you a referral, they can be amazing referral sources since they are in front of your clients on a regular basis.

Knowing who is in your contact sphere takes some work. You have to know who your potential clients are, also known as your target markets. Once you determine your target markets, you can identify other businesses that would also want to work with those customers.

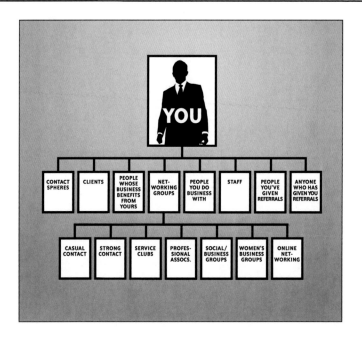

People often limit themselves to certain industries to develop contact spheres. For instance, a real estate agent may look to develop relationships with a mortgage loan officer, a title company, a home insurance company, and a home inspector. These are all logical, because they all work in the residential housing industry.

But what if the real estate agent has a niche market? What if she primarily sells condominiums to retired people? Using her niche market, she may be better off partnering with businesses that target the elderly, like hearing aid stores, dance studios, travel agents, or Medicare supplement insurance agents. You have to think about who your customers are and then figure out what other businesses work with those same people.

The concept of target marketing is foreign to many people. They think they need to be all things to all people, and that anyone would be a good customer for them. But identifying a target market allows you to select other potential business partners who share your customers.

#2 – Clients

When was the last time you asked your clients for a referral? Most of the time we don't do it because we are scared that we haven't done enough for them to motivate them properly. That much could be true. We need to find ways to help our clients more.

What if you called your client Joe Smith and asked for an appointment to sit down and figure out a way to help promote his business? What do you think his reaction would be? At first, he may think there is some kind of catch, as though you are trying a backdoor approach to sell him something. Once he realizes that you genuinely are trying to help him, he may find you much more credible.

Has anyone ever asked you to meet and talk about growing your business? How would you react to that kind of request? Would you think more highly of someone who asked you that question and who genuinely wanted to help you?

Pick two of your clients who you think will be great referral sources for your business. If these clients are in your contact sphere, even better. Ask them for a one-on-one meeting to help grow their business and see how they respond.

If you focus on helping others, they will want to help you. Dale Carnegie said about being successful, "All you have to do is help other people achieve their goals." Do you know what your clients' goals are? If you help them meet their goals, they will be more inclined to want to help you. The worst that could happen is you establish a better relationship with your clients by getting to know them better.

#3 – People whose business benefits from yours

There are certain companies that get more business when you get more business. Suppose you are a printer who specializes in wedding invitations. Every time you get a new customer, you may need to order more paper, ink, ribbon, contact paper, etc. The businesses that provide those supplies to you get more business, because you get more business.

Have you ever talked to your suppliers about helping them with their businesses? You may be a great referral source for them if you are already using their products. If you develop relationships with your vendors and motivate them to refer you business, they could be great referral sources for you.

#4 – Networking Groups

Earlier in this book, I mentioned three major types of networking groups with which you can get involved. But actually, you can become active in another four types. Following are all seven types of networking groups:

- Casual contact
- Strong/Hard-contact
- Service clubs
- Professional associations

- Social business groups
- Women's groups
- Online networking

You should select networking groups that you are interested in getting involved with and to which you feel you can dedicate time. I recommend being visible and active in your networking groups so that you can build long-term credibility. Select three groups and work to develop relationships. Find people within each of the groups who are in your contact sphere, so you can determine if they would be long-term referral sources.

#5 – People with whom you do business

Here's an easy one: follow your money. To whom are you currently writing checks or swiping your credit card? When was the last time you asked for a referral from your insurance person, banker, or CPA?

Ask the people with whom you do business, especially if they are in your contact sphere, if they would like to explore a referral relationship. If they say no, you may want to think about changing providers. This is not always the case, but it is a good idea to be out in the open with your service providers. If you don't change, at least you know not to expect any referrals from them.

We must all strive to have mutually beneficial relationships in our network. If you are referring someone, that person should be willing to refer you. If you are using someone's services and he or she is not referring you, and you have had the open conversation about starting a referral relationship, I would not refer any business to that person.

#6 – Employees

Do your employees know that they need to find referrals for you? Do your employees carry your business card with them at all times? Do they know your business, and are you doing what is necessary to motivate them to refer business to you?

You might assume that your staff is equipped to give you referrals. Unfortunately, this is not always the case. Just because you provide people with paychecks does not mean they will provide you referrals. They expect you to pay them, so you are not going above and beyond to motivate them properly.

In most companies, the #1 salesperson is the receptionist. This person knows how to promote your business better than anyone else. Receptionists understand how it works, and they talk to all your prospects and clients. This person could either work for you or against you, depending on how you treat her.

I know of a successful financial advisor who never got referrals from his receptionist. The reason? His receptionist was good friends with another financial advisor, so she sent all of her friends and family to the other advisor! Her boss was writing her paycheck, but he had not educated her on why he needed to receive the referrals over this other person.

Take the time to educate and motivate your staff to understand why referrals are important, and determine how you can help them. Make them partners in your business growth by sharing ways they can help you. All you may have to do is ask, and you will begin receiving referrals from your employees.

#7 – People you have given referrals to in the past

You may have referred business to people over the years and lost touch with them. These people may still remember you, even decades after you sent them the referrals, depending on how good the referral was. If you reconnect with them, these people are possible sources who may be willing to repay you with referrals.

#8 – People to whom you currently give referrals

People you currently refer business to should be motivated to give you referrals in return. Hopefully you have existing relationships with people who are referring business back to you.

The goal is to bring at least four people to Profitability in the VCP Process® before you attempt to bring on additional referral partners. In order to build a multi-million dollar business, you only need between four and eight quality referral sources.

Do you think it is far-fetched to build a successful business with only eight referral partners? A referral partner is someone who is willing to send you referrals week in and week out. Think about this: if each of those eight people send you only one referral per week, that is 416 referrals in a year. How would your business look with an additional 416 referrals?

You must find four people who are truly motivated to find referrals for you. If one of the people you currently have identified as a possible source cannot give you many referrals, find someone else who can. Go through your database and filter it based on who would fit into the above eight categories. Once you find the first four, move on to the next four, and you will build a successful referral business. Keep in mind: you must always be motivating your referral partners if you want them to continually give you business.

CHAPTER ELEVEN

BUILD A REFERRAL BANK ACCOUNT

With the first four people you identify as potential referral sources, start to plant the seed for them to give you referrals in the future. The best way to do that is to develop a referral bank account with each of these people. This will allow you to ask them for referrals at some point.

Have you ever tried to withdraw money from your checking account when there was no money in it? How well did that work? You must have money in your checking account in order to make withdrawals. You need to make deposits first.

The same goes for referral relationships. You have to make deposits into someone's referral bank account in order for you to make withdrawals by asking for referrals.

I know what you might be asking yourself: "I can't give my clients referrals, so how am I going to make deposits into their referral bank accounts?" Take the referral blinders off. You have additional ways to get a referral than by giving someone a referral first.

In their book *Business by Referral,* Dr. Ivan Misner and Robert Davis identify 18 ways to motivate referral sources. One of them is giving them a referral. You have 17 other ways to motivate someone to give you a referral that have nothing to do with you giving a referral first.

Here is an example: let's suppose you are an insurance agent, and your #1 referral source is a housewife whose husband is retired. There is no referral you can give her to motivate her, and you are not allowed to spend any money on her. We've already said you need the relationship to continue to be profitable or else the referrals will dry up. What can you do?

You may think that thanking her for her referrals is good enough. Always send a thank you note and always follow up on the referrals. This is good practice, but it does not qualify as motivating someone, because it is expected.

What if you were to volunteer your time doing something that is important to her? Suppose she is passionate about animals and spends a lot of time at a local animal rescue. You could ask to attend a fundraiser and help her setup tables, clean animal cages or walk some of the dogs. Do you think she would find value in this? Volunteering would be a deposit into the housewife's referral bank account. This is just one of the ways to motivate someone to give you referrals. Take the referral blinders off.

Suppose you are a mortgage loan officer, and real estate agents are your number one referral source. It would make sense to have more than one real estate agent referring you business. You may be wondering how you can have a referral relationship with more than one real estate agent. How would you know to whom to give the referral?

Take the referral blinders off and think about the bank account. What else could you do to make deposits into each real estate agent's bank account? Could you invite her to a networking event or nominate her for a service award? Find out what is important to your referral sources and you will tap into the other ways you can motivate them besides giving them referrals.

REVIEW: STEP TWO

STEP TWO: Have the Right Vehicle

- Pick the Right Vehicle
- Referrals
- Predicting Referrals
- The VCP Process®
- Eight Sources of Referrals
- Build a Referral Bank Account

POINTS TO PONDER:

Are you receiving all the referrals you want?

_____

_____

_____

_____

What do you currently do when you receive a bad referral?

_____

_____

_____

_____

Identify networking groups in which you are currently involved from the three major categories.

- Hard-contact
- Casual contact
- Service club

Are you getting referrals from your clients?

_____

_____

_____

_____

Where are you in the VCP Process® with your clients and referral sources?

_____

_____

_____

_____

Have you explored the eight sources of referrals for more potential referral partners?

_____

_____

_____

_____

Think about ways to motivate your referral sources besides giving them referrals.

_____

_____

_____

_____

STEP THREE:

BE CONSISTENT

CHAPTER TWELVE

OUTSTANDING TRAINING = OUTSTANDING LIFE

In order to achieve your personal, financial, and referral marketing goals, you must have quality training that matches what you aspire to be. Quality training helps you build and maintain a strong foundation in whatever you are doing so you can be consistent.

Most training programs are good, but they're ordinary, which is fine if you just want to be ordinary. If you want to be outstanding, you must immerse and engage in outstanding training.

There are four things a training company must do in order to have outstanding training. If any one of the four is missing, it's less than outstanding. A training system must:

1. **Create habits**

2. **Provide accountability**

3. **Deliver coaching and mentoring**

4. **Be simple and duplicable.**

A training program must create habits, which is why the majority of programs don't work. You might attend a training and get jazzed up for a few weeks about what you learned, and then you go back to doing the things you have always done. The program has to eliminate your old habits and properly instill new ones.

You also must have accountability with a training program. You have to be accountable to yourself and to a system. The training company has to be accountable as well. Many training companies will hold you accountable, but you often can't hold them accountable.

Accountability often comes in the form of coaching and mentoring. People throw in the towel when things get rough. A coach helps push you along to help break your old habits and reinforce the new ones. It's easy to have an ordinary life. Anyone can be ordinary. To have an outstanding life, we must stretch beyond what was previously thought possible. Coaches and mentors provide guidance and support to help us achieve more.

Learning a new system can be daunting, so a training program must be simple and duplicable. Have you ever picked up a book that promised an "easy to follow" system, and the book was 450 pages long? How easy can that be?

Of the four components, the most important is creating habits. In order to get different results, we have to do things differently, which requires breaking old habits and creating new ones.

New skills we learn in training can become rooted if we do them consistently. This is important in referral marketing because much of what people learn about referral marketing is different from how they are presently advertising and marketing their business. Old habits must be broken and new habits adopted.

CHAPTER THIRTEEN

BREAKING AND CREATING HABITS

Did you know that in space everything appears to be upside down? NASA scientists worried how their astronauts, who would spend 2-3 weeks at a time in the space station, would handle this type of environment. Would the astronauts be disoriented, unable to perform in outer space?

So NASA had a group of astronauts wear special goggles continuously for extended periods of time. The goggles inverted all images, so the world looked upside down, simulating the conditions on the space station. While wearing their goggles, astronauts were asked to reach down; however, they would actually reach up due to the goggles' image inversion.

Something interesting happened to every person in the study group which the NASA scientists didn't expect. A change occurred on the 25th day of wearing the goggles.

Before this discovery, NASA was unaware of the possibility of this happening.

On the 25th day, each astronaut's mind automatically inverted the image in the goggles. Thus, when the astronauts reached down to grab something, they were actually reaching in the same direction they saw. The scientists had the astronauts remove their goggles for 24 hours and then wear them again. What do you think happened?

The images were again reversed. The astronauts had to wear the goggles for another 25-30 days for their minds to automatically invert the images again.

It takes 25-30 days to establish a habit. This is why weight loss programs and smoking cessation plans don't work. If you go off a diet for one day, you need another 25 days to get back. If you quit smoking and then have one cigarette, you go back to the beginning.

Creating habits is hard, which is why a mentor is so important. You need to find a good role model that will keep you accountable, give you positive input, is compatible with you, and will give you a system that you can emulate.

When you find a good mentor, simply copy what she does. If you are a financial planner and want to be the best, find the best and do exactly what he does. If they get into the office at 6am to plan their day, you are in your office at 6am planning your day. If they exercise for an hour every day before lunch, you exercise for an hour. If they go to Starbucks at 8:15am, you go to Starbucks at 8:15am. You get the idea.

You emulate your role model because whatever they are doing works. Follow someone who is where you want to be in life and do what they do. You've heard the saying "you can't know what it feels to be like someone until you walk a mile in his shoes." Go walk a mile in his shoes. I am serious. Wear the same shoes he wears and buy them from the same store. (Okay, this may be overboard, but seriously, emulate your mentor!)

The challenge is finding someone to emulate who is really great.. Many people are successful but have no idea what they are doing. A mentor must be able to communicate the system she is using in order for you to duplicate her success.

You must find a training system and a role model that you can identify with, so you can learn to do the right thing — consistently.

REVIEW: Step Three

STEP THREE: Be Consistent

- Outstanding Training = Outstanding Life
- Breaking and Creating Habits

POINTS TO PONDER:

Is the current training you are engaged in outstanding or ordinary? _____

_____

_____

_____

What are some habits you would like to break?

_____

_____

_____

_____

What are some new habits you would like to create?

_____

_____

_____

_____

Who is a mentor you could follow and emulate?

_____

"What would you do if you knew you could not fail?"
— Robert H. Schuller

STEP FOUR

BE PERSISTENT

Chapter Fourteen

Set the Right Goals

What would you do if you knew you could not fail? Would you dream bigger? Is it even possible to fail?

Many people never try for fear of failure. But the only way to fail is to never try or try and give up. I'll repeat that: the only way to fail is to give up.

Do you see what is wrong in this picture? The workers

are putting in new posts on this corner to prevent vehicles from crashing into the building. One of the guys gets into the truck to leave, but the truck is inside the barriers they have just installed. They can't get out. They have to tear down the posts and finish the job from the outside.

Sometimes this happens when you try to achieve your goals. Either you put up your own obstacles or you have to break through obstacles that appear. When obstacles appear, what do you do?

The best thing to do is to tear the obstacles down and get back to what you were trying to accomplish. We will always have things blocking our way when we try to achieve goals. Other people, money, and frustration can all impact how quickly we get to our destination. We must be persistent if we want to accomplish what we set out to do.

Read *Think and Grow Rich* by Napoleon Hill, written in 1937. Napoleon Hill said, "Whatever the mind can conceive and believe, it can achieve."

Set at least one goal to be the ultimate goal in your life when you accomplish it. Napoleon Hill said if you do this, you will eventually hit that goal.

Most of us don't commit ourselves to big goals. We tend to make our goals too easy. We need to have goals that are attainable and a bit of a stretch, but we have to have one that is HUGE. We need one that is way outside that box that really drives us to strive for more than we ever thought ourselves capable of achieving.

Hill also said you can't have negative goals. Rather than say, "I want to lose weight," say, "I want a new look."

Instead of "I want to get out of debt," say, "I want financial freedom." Focus on the positive aspects of what you are trying to achieve rather than the negative elements you are eliminating.

In his book, *Remember the Ice*, Bob Nicoll recounts his experience working with a convenience store owner in Phoenix, Arizona. The store owner was complaining about his ice sales. This was in the summer, when Arizona is routinely hotter than 100 degrees Fahrenheit.

REMEMBER THE ICE
AND OTHER PARADIGM SHIFTS

BOB NICOLL, MA

Bob knew what the problem was. He suggested to the owner that he change a sign that read "Don't Forget the Ice!" to "Remember the Ice!"

Bob Nicoll is the Chief Paradigm Shifter for Remember the Ice, LLC, 12043 Town Park Circle, Eagle River, AK 99577 · 907-862-1983 · www.remembertheice.com

Bob came back to the store a few days later and asked the owner how business was, and specifically, how his ice sales were going. The store owner said he could barely keep the ice in stock, because he was selling so much. All because he reframed his message to focus on the positive rather than the negative.

Your mind will reject negative goals. It is important to set positive goals and to remember that it takes 25-30 days to create a habit.

CHAPTER FIFTEEN

VISUALIZE YOUR GOALS

In order for your mind to accept that a goal is real, you have to create a visual representation of your goal. If you create something you can touch or see every day, your mind will begin to accept the goal, and it will be easier for you to work toward it. Writing down your goals is the first step to making them happen.

Have you heard of Jack Canfield, author of *Chicken Soup for the Soul*? Jack was turned down by a multitude of publishers. Most said that no one would buy a book titled *Chicken Soup for the Soul*.

But one publisher had faith in him. That book has sold more than 100 million copies, and Jack Canfield and his business partner, Mark Victor Hansen, have recently struck a deal in China to translate their bestselling book series into Chinese. With more than 1 billion people in China, *Chicken Soup for the Soul* will surely set sales and distribution records. It will likely become one of the bestselling books of all time, second only to the Bible.

In his 20s, Jack hooked up with a mentor who told him to set a goal that was outside the box. Jack decided he wanted to make $100,000 the next year.

At the time, he was making about $8,000 per year as a schoolteacher. His mentor told him to get a picture of a $100,000 bill and put it on the ceiling above his bed.

That $100,000 bill was the first thing he saw in the morning and the last thing he saw at night. Every night before bed and each morning when he awoke, Jack said out loud, "I am going to make $100,000 this year."

Do you know how much money Jack Canfield made that year? Just a little less than $100,000. Do you think he was happy with that number? Happy, but not satisfied. He was close to his goal that year and is a multimillionaire today.

Jack proved that you have to see your goals to make them happen. As much as you can touch and feel your goals, that will help you in your journey. If there is a house you want to buy, go tour it. If there is a car you want, go test drive it. If you have a dream vacation you want to take, go see a travel agent and plan it. Every time you want to quit, go tour the house, test drive the car, or go see the travel agent.

Maybe you have a goal to donate $1,000,000 to charity. You need to visualize it. Picture the day you are going to do it and write it down. Actually write out a check for $1,000,000 in the name of a charity and post it somewhere visible on your desk or wall.

Maybe you want to start a foundation to provide scholarships for needy kids. Visualize the checks all over your desk made out to each of the kids who will benefit from your endowment.

Make a vision board and post your goals on it. Put it somewhere you can see it before you go to bed and when you wake up, just like Jack Canfield. Who knows what will happen?

CHAPTER SIXTEEN

BROADCAST YOUR GOALS

If you want to achieve your goals, you have to broadcast them. Tell as many people as you can what your goals are. Most people don't share their goals with others, and in some ways, it makes the goals less real.

Do you know why people don't share their goals? Because they don't know what they are! Many people have never taken the time to think about the goals they have for the future. So there is no chance they will tell others. Some people are too scared that if they tell someone about their goals, they will actually have to do some work to accomplish them. They would rather be without that responsibility.

In the upcoming space provided, write down five of your goals. Many people are unable to do this, because they are unaware of what their goals are. They live day-to-day and can't get beyond that mindset. They are in a rut and don't know their goals.

For the first goal, write down how much you want to increase your income in the next twelve months. Most people never write down this kind of goal. They say, "I want to be more successful or make more money," but you have to quantify it. If you want to double or triple your income, write this down.

For the second goal, specify how many hours per week you want to work. I recommend, assuming you want to work less than you are now, to write down a number that is lower than what you are currently working. If you are working 80 hours per week, you might write down 60. If you are working 40 hours per week, you might write down 30. With well trained referral partners, it is possible to work less and make more. Too many people set goals and then work harder to achieve them. You have to work smarter.

For the last three of the five, set goals that are longer term, with one of them being WAY outside the box — something you may have never thought possible but would be a dream come true. This is the goal that will motivate you every day to do what you need to do to accomplish more.

This is not a book about goals, but you must have goals if you want your referral marketing to kick in to overdrive. Write your five below. You must be very specific about what you want. General goals will never happen, because our minds are unable to visualize them happening.

Goals:

1. _____

2. _____

3. _____

4. _____

5. _____

Now, photocopy this page and keep these goals somewhere you can see them. Better yet, post them where others can see them, on your fridge, at your desk, on your car window, on your forehead, whatever. You have to tell someone else who will hold you accountable to meeting these goals. Someone who can check in with you on a regular basis and ask you how you are doing with your goals.

Do you know who the #1 motivator for completing goals is? Children, especially your own. Tell your children that when you reach your goal something great will happen, like going to Disneyworld for two weeks. But it is only going to happen if you are able to reach your goals.

If you have a morning in which you don't feel like getting out of bed or putting in the extra hours to hit your goals, your 5 year old is going to tell you to get your butt out of bed, because she wants to go to Disneyworld! You need motivators, and kids work great for this.

Kids are great at holding us accountable to big goals, because they believe anything is possible. They have yet to be programmed that it is possible to fail.

"If we all did the things we are capable of doing, we would literally astound ourselves."
— Thomas Edison

CHAPTER SEVENTEEN

CAN YOU FAIL?

What is Thomas Edison's most famous invention? The light bulb. Actually, he did not invent the light bulb, but he is typically credited with it. In fact, Thomas Edison made the light bulb commercially viable through his experimentation. Did you know that he had 10,000 attempts before producing a satisfactory light bulb?

In the early days of electricity, Thomas Edison had to travel to promote the light bulb at press conferences. He was in a roomful of reporters telling them about his great invention. A reporter from the back of the room stood up and challenged him, saying, "Thomas Edison, how dare you gloat. How dare you tell us how great you are! I know for a fact that you had 10,000 experimental failures before you invented that light bulb. I want you to justify that to the world."

The room went silent, and Thomas Edison thought about the reporter's statement for what seemed like five minutes. Staring back at the reporter, he finally replied, "Young man, I did not have 10,000 experimental failures in that light bulb. I found 10,000 different ways that a light bulb did not work."

Thomas Edison never failed. He simply found methods that produced nonworking inventions. He learned something each time one of his inventions didn't work. He had the persistence required to keep going until he had something that did work.

It's easy to give up and hard to be persistent. I get it. But those who believe in themselves and do whatever they can to achieve their goals will be successful in the end.

Have you ever given up too early, seeing in hindsight that if you stuck with it just a bit longer everything would have worked out? You end up like a marathon runner sitting out the last mile. As the saying goes, sometimes it is hard to see the forest for the trees.

When we are in difficult situations, it is often easier to give up than to stay the course. But just like Edison, each time we try we learn something new that may take us even further than we ever thought possible. What will be your "light bulb"?

How badly do you want to achieve your goals? Did you arrive at your goals because someone told you goals are important, or is there something inside of you that is pushing you to achieve more? If your goals are truly a part of your being, you will do all you can to achieve them. Be persistent and your work will pay off.

REVIEW: Step Four

STEP FOUR: Be Persistent
- Set the Right Goals
- Visualize Your Goals
- Broadcast Your Goals
- Can You Fail?

POINTS TO PONDER:

What is your ultimate stretch goal? _____

_____

_____

_____

Of your current goals, on which ones can you put a positive spin? _____

_____

_____

Create a vision board for one of your goals. Include:

_____

_____

_____

Who is an accountability partner to whom you could broadcast your goals? _____

_____

CHAPTER EIGHTEEN

THAT'S IT?

"The simplest things are often the truest."
— Richard Bach

1. **Believe in yourself**
2. **Drive the right vehicle**
3. **Be consistent**
4. **Be persistent**

That's it. That's all there is. Four amazingly simple steps to personal, financial, and referral marketing success. Life is way too complex already. So now that I've made it easy for you to have success in your life, will you give it your best shot?

I know if you follow this system, you will find success in whatever you do. This system has helped me achieve great things in my life, and I know it can help you.

To your success,

Tim R. Green

IT'S YOUR CHOICE

"We make choices every day about what will inspire us and what we will allow to get us down. We have a choice to move ahead or allow ourselves to stay stuck in a rut.

We have the power to let go, the power to hang on and the power to be: be all of who we were designed to be. We have our authentic selves that continue to evolve and emerge each day through every experience."
— Lisa Mininni

You make choices every day. Today you have a choice on whether or not you will change what you're doing right now and embrace what you've learned. It's no mistake that you received this book at just the right time. With every book you read, there is a message in it for you. Over the years, I've come to realize that we receive messages.

And here's the crossroads where people get stuck, even though they are getting these messages. Not only do they get stuck, they fail to even try a different way of doing things: this is called apathy.

71

The journey to apathy often comes out of a constant struggle for clarity of direction. One day you find yourself at a crossroads, because you feel that you've "tried everything" and "nothing" seems to be working! You're confused about your direction and start that internal conversation, "maybe I'm not meant to have the same lifestyle I did before." "Maybe I'm not as good as I think I am as a small business owner." "I just don't know if I can continue with owning my own business." These self-limiting conversations leave the entrepreneur stuck more than a horse in a mud pit. (And if you've ever seen a horse in a mud pit, you know what I mean.)

One thing is certain. Each small business owner has a present and a future. Everything in between is the process. If you're struggling with your business, Tim Green artfully describes the essential ingredients to a successful referral system that can change your business and your life.

It's up to you to do something with it and move from apathy to accomplishment. Even though your present situation may not be where you want it to be, there's good news. There's a way out of the stuck place of apathy.

You've received four powerful steps toward personal, financial and referral success. And now here is your choice to move ahead. So how does a small business owner choose to move from apathy to accomplishment?

FOUR MORE SIMPLE STEPS:

1. Embrace Powerful Choices

As I mention in *Me, Myself, and Why? The Secrets to Navigating Change*, "We make choices every day about what will inspire us and what we will allow to get us down. We have a choice to move ahead or allow ourselves to stay stuck in a rut." I have noticed that effective business owners make good choices, and their choices are enhanced by their level of awareness about themselves. Awareness pushes a small business owner beyond any self-limiting comfort zone. The most powerful is the choice of whether or not you will choose to have PAAR (power, accountability, authority and responsibility) over the results you intend to achieve and the life you want to lead.

If you don't think you have a choice, (and think you lack personal power to change your circumstances) your self-limiting actions will follow. Successful entrepreneurs choose and use their personal PAAR to move beyond any feelings of powerlessness or apathy.

2. Create Your Vision

The most successful leaders even in the most desperate times created a vision for the future. They consistently spoke that vision and engendered that vision in others. This creative power of vision overcomes apathy when you can imagine an ideal future. When you start imagining your ideal future, you use your imagination to build on your innate strengths and motivations that overcome often irrational fears.

Once you create your vision, start speaking it. Identify goals, implement new learning, write down your list of things you intend to attract in your life, and take action. It's amazing what you attract when you speak your vision, engender that vision in others and start taking action based on each new nugget you learn.

3. Recognize the Power of Positive Thought

Have you ever known someone who sapped your energy? Conversely, have you known someone who was an energizer and made you feel good when you were around them? Chances are, the energizer had a positive outlook and was often focused on the strengths of others or made it a point to help others. But if you're in apathy, you're likely focused on yourself and your own problems.

When you shift to positive thought, several things will happen:

· It Boosts Your Self Confidence. Self-confidence makes doing business with you attractive.

· You Attract Your Ideal. When you're focused on what it is you do intend to attract, you'll invite more of it into your life and your business.

· You Attract More Business. When you focus on the strengths of others, helping others, and display a positive self-image, it engages interest from others. People enjoy being around people who generate creative ideas, not only for themselves, but for others around them. You become a trusted source and people send others they know to you.

4. Choose Courage

Choose emotional courage even in the face of adversity. Responding to adversity with positive actions rather than negative beliefs will get you further ahead. At first, it may be difficult to overcome the proposal you lost or the deal that never went through. Savvy business owners know they have the choice of responding with positive actions and every time they do it, it further develops their emotional courage.

Exercise Your Courage:

- Take Imperfect Action. The more you take, the more you build up your capacity. Start with a concept from this book that you understood really well and try it out. Don't even try to be perfect at it – just try it without putting any judgment on it. Taking small steps of imperfect action creates giant leaps later.

- Consciously Choose to Act Courageously. The fear of failure causes many small business owners to blame or procrastinate then rationalize those excuses. After all, you can't lose a game you never play, right? So entrepreneurs remove themselves from ever playing. To develop emotional courage, make a shift. Instead of talking yourself out of not playing next time, redesign your attitude, and, in its place, define what you can do, rather than rationalizing what you can't do.

The next time you feel the weight of apathy enveloping you, cancel it. You now have the tools to change your future. Choose to believe that you have the power to let go of what weighs you down, the power to change your current reality and the power to be: be all of who you were designed to be.

Lisa Mininni is a Referral Institute, Referrals for Life® Student and President of Excellerate Associates, home of The Entrepreneurial Edge System™, the only national developmental and marketing program showing small business owners how their clients find them, choose them, and buy from them, filling their business in record time. To discover how to put your business goals on the fast track, visit http://www.freebusinessplanformat.com.

APPENDIX

REFERRAL INSTITUTE

The Referral Institute was founded in 1999 by Dr. Ivan Misner. Seeing the need for additional referral marketing training, Dr. Ivan Misner began cultivating material that would train business professionals to implement specific procedures on referral based marketing. Dr. Misner's many bestselling books on the subject led to creating Certified Networker®, a 12-module training program that allows participants to receive the foundational knowledge they need for a referral marketing plan for their business. Over time, the company began developing additional customized programs on referral marketing techniques.

The Referral Institute is one of the fastest growing franchises in the world. In fact, Entrepreneur.com has listed the Referral Institute in its annual top 500 franchises four years in a row (2007-2010).

The mission of the Referral Institute is to help people create Referrals For Life®.

Referral marketing has three core competencies:

1. People must have the RIGHT referral marketing knowledge.

2. Students need to stay immersed in the information and implement their referral plan.

3. Students' referral networks need to be trained properly by experts.

The program that brought all of these items together for Referral Institute clients is the "Referrals For Life®" program. This program allows students to spend a minimum of one year attending any or *all* of the Referral Institute programs. It also provides several opportunities to bring their referral network to the experts to be trained. Most importantly, the student stays immersed in the material, basically guaranteeing implementation of the material into their business.

The Referral For Life® program consists of three core programs: Certified Networker® II, Roomful of Referrals™ and Referral Pipeline™.

Certified Networker® II

The Certified Networker II program is ideal for small business owners and sales professionals who have grown weary of time and cost-intensive lead acquisition and cold calling. Participants learn how to dramatically improve sales prospecting efficiency with proven referral marketing approaches.

The program's customized curriculum is designed to provide business professionals with tips, tools and techniques to help them become more effective and productive business networkers. In addition, all participants leave the program with their own customized referral-based marketing business plan.

The Certified Networker II is taught in a series of 12 interactive modules designed to give participants a complete overview of the referral marketing process, along with requisite skills and a plan that ensures success.

Module 1: Finding Your Starting Point

Understand your business and reasons customers choose you or your business over your competitors.

Module 2: Identifying Your Networks and Using the VCP Process®

Your relationships pass through three phases to play a role in building your business.

Module 3: The 10 Commandments of Networking a Mixer

You will never find a business mixer to be a waste of time again when you learn how to effectively network at these events.

Module 4: Making Introductions That Last

Ensuring that your referral sources remember and reward you.

Module 5: Creating and Delivering an Effective Presentation

Deliver your presentation with style and confidence; learn how to give an effective 10-12 minute presentation.

Module 6: Tools and Techniques for Enhancing Your Business Image

Designing and assembling an image that generates qualified referrals.

Module 7: Contact Spheres, Hub Firms, Mining a Vein and 7 Different Types of Business Organizations

Understand the concept of a hub firm, develop an understanding to mine a "vein" for referrals, and learn the seven types of networking groups

Module 8: The GAINS Profile and 15 Ways to Promote

Develop relationships you have already identified as potential sources of referrals and learn to use the GAINS Profile.

Module 9: 18 Tactics to Motivate Your Referral Partners

Motivate your networking sources to establish and develop a business relationship.

Module 10: Training Your Referral Partners

Referral marketing; you can't do it alone. What does your referral partner need to know?

Module 11: Evaluating Your Effectiveness, "It's all my fault."

Developing a system for tracking your referral sources and quality of referrals.

Module 12: Generating Referrals For Life®

Learn how to effectively ask for referrals and reward those who give them to you.

Roomful of Referrals™

This workshop will teach you how to quickly recognize the behavioral "style" of anyone. Armed with this knowledge, you'll be able to adapt your own communication style to quickly establish rapport and trust...with nearly anyone. This information will also help you to become a master networker. Discover how to leverage behavioral styles to make networking pay off in tangible business results for you.

Referral Pipeline™

A one-day seminar in which participants learn about a powerful yet easy referral process and actually leave with scheduled appointments. When was the last time you went to a seminar and walked away with business?

At the Referral Institute, we not only show salespeople and business owners how to fill their sales pipeline, we also jump-start the process. On the day of training, participants actually schedule appointments with qualified prospects. And it's easy!

Of course, we provide valuable information about our referral process during the one-day seminar. However, the focus of our program is on having you participate in the process. So you not only learn about it, you have firsthand experience with it.

Pipeline Seminar participants use the RISE2™ strategy to Identify, Strategize and Execute a process that will efficiently generate enough referrals to completely fill up their sales pipeline!

In order to make this training and your time more effective, all participants are required to attend this training with a trusted member from their network and to bring their contact list, address book or electronic database. The investment in this program covers the fees for BOTH participants. Working together as a team of two, you will learn the RISE2™ process and how to generate more and better referrals for each other.

The organization continues to grow 100% by referral. In fact, in order to be involved with our company, you must be referred! Yet, whether you are in Australia, Canada, Germany, Ireland, New Zealand, the United Kingdom, Norway, Finland, Denmark, Sweden, Middle East or the United States, the Referral Institute has material to help all professional business owners create MORE business by referral. As we continue to coach our clients, add new training programs, and offer customized consulting, you can be assured that the Referral Institute will be in the forefront of proactive referral strategies for its clients. We look forward to seeing you at the next program!

To contact Referral Institute, send an email to info@ referralinstitute.com or call 707-780-8110. Key Executives of the Referral Institute include: Ivan R. Misner, Ph.D., Senior Partner and Michael Macedonio, Partner & President.

ABOUT THE AUTHOR

TIM R. GREEN

As an inspirational and motivational speaker, Tim has a gift for taking complex strategies, such as becoming an expert in referral marketing, and making them simple to implement. He has traveled coast to coast motivating and inspiring audiences of 5,000 plus.

Tim has recently presented for numerous corporations and organizations, including the Michigan Jaycees State Convention, Automation Alley in Troy, Vistage (formerly TEC Associates), and several Michigan Real Estate Boards and Real Estate offices. Tim was also a featured speaker at Referrals for Life® Day and Referral Institute's International Convention.

Who do you know who is looking for a

referral marketing expert to present to

their organization or company?

Referral Institute of Michigan offers three one hour presentations to organizations and companies:

· "Take Referral Marketing to the Extreme"

· "Getting Emotional about Referral Marketing"

· "Let's get Personal with our Referral Source & Clients."

If you refer us to an organization, we will promote you in our presentation. If granted permission by the sponsoring company, we will give you a list of the attendees to contact after the presentation.

What are they saying about Tim?

"Tim Green can truly inspire and motivate a crowd, and his knowledge on referral marketing training is no less than outstanding. I have seen many, many presentations over the years, and Tim is in a class of his own as a presenter. I consider him to be one of our number one referral marketing trainers at Referral Institute. No matter how many times I see him speak, he never fails to impress me with his dynamic ability to capture an audience."

Ivan Misner, NY Times Bestselling author and Founder of Referral Institute

"I want to congratulate you again on the sensational speech you gave at the Referral Institute Conference in New Orleans last month. As a professional conference speaker and the International President of the Global Speakers Federation, I get to see a lot of speakers deliver presentations all around the world. Your presentation is one of the most inspiring and motivating presentations I have seen in a long time."

Lindsay Adams CSP
President, Global Speakers Federation
Nevin Award Winner
Past National President, National Speakers
Association of Australia

"I've met and spoken with many top speakers, NY Times Bestselling authors, and media celebrities in the last five years in my travels. Tim ranks right up there with the best I've ever seen."

Tony Rubleski #1 Amazon Bestselling Author
President, Mind Capture Group
www.MindCaptureGroup.com

CONTACT US

Your Name: _____

Your Phone Number: _____

Your Email: _____

Organization/Business: _____

_____

One of our staff members will contact you to arrange a meeting with the organization or business.

4381 Davison Rd., Burton, MI 48509

Phone 877-241-3577 · Fax 810-715-2569

Karen Green – Karen@RIofMI.com

www.RIofMI.com

be referred! Yet, whether you are in Australia, Canada, Germany, Ireland, New Zealand, the United Kingdom, Norway, Finland, Denmark, Sweden, Middle East or the United States, the Referral Institute has material to help all professional business owners create MORE business by referral. As we continue to coach our clients, add new training programs, and offer customized consulting, you can be assured that the Referral Institute will be in the forefront of proactive referral strategies for its clients. We look forward to seeing you at the next program!

To contact Referral Institute, send an email to info@ referralinstitute.com or call 707-780-8110. Key Executives of the Referral Institute include: Ivan R. Misner, Ph.D., Senior Partner and Michael Macedonio, Partner & President.